LUPUS LOVE

by Tammy Anderson
illustrated by Claude E. Daniel

Moral Literature™

Dedicated To
SABAR
and
to all the little angels that
love someone with Lupus

Text 2008 Tammy Anderson

All rights reserved. For information about permission
to reproduce selections from this book please contact Tammy Anderson
@ Moraliterature@yahoo.com

Library of Congress Cataloging-in-Publication Data

Anderson Tammy
Lupus Love: A story of love / Tammy Anderson

ISBN - (Paperback) 978-1-4528-3245-6

Manufactured in the United States of America

Copyright © Moral Literature , Tammy Anderson 2008
THE MORAL LITERATURE'S logos and word mark are trademarks of Moral Litera-
ture. Inc

Summary: Lupus Love is a child friendly piece of literature that will assist in the ex-
planation of the ups and downs of an individual suffering from SLE.

Visit us or contact us on the Web: www.lupuslove.org

Tammy Anderson
Moraliterature@yahoo.com

Claude E. Daniel
Paradoxunlimited@yahoo.com

Moral Literature Children's Books supports the First Amendment and celebrates the
right to read.

TM *and © 2008*

My Mommy has lupus but I can't see. On the outside she looks very normal to me!

Now that Mommy has lupus things have changed. Some of the family fun has been rearranged.

During the summer our family has lots of fun.
Planning, playing, and vacationing in the sun.

But now that mommy has lupus, she can't stay out long. The sun makes her tired and she has to go home.

But I just whisper, " It's okay mommy. You can't be in the sun. We can play on the inside which is just as much fun."

I like for mommy to come when we have field trips at school Because my friends thinks she's really, really cool!

Now that mommy has lupus walking a short distance can be tough. During the field trip it's a little hard to keep up.

Sometimes in the group she may fall behind.
I turn around and she's missing from the field trip line!

"What's wrong with your mommy?" my friends ask me
"She has lupus", I say, "something we can't see."

Oh boy! But watch out when mommy has a good day.
All my friends come over and they all beg to stay!

After a long day mommy is sleeping I see daddy closing the door. I sneak inside to be close to her and sit quietly on the floor.

I look at my mother and see her struggle. She tries so hard to take care of me and my busy little brother.

So I step up and lend a helping hand When or wherever I possibly can.

There are times when I ask my friend Nicky,
"Why is my Mommy's lupus so, so, so, tricky?"

Nicky is a good friend for me to talk to.
Her mom has lupus long before my mother knew.

I asked her, "How can mommy have trouble walking
sometimes But later that day she's walking just fine? "

Or why is it that the rain
brings mommy a little or a lot of pain?

And, why does mommy sometimes stay in bed all
day And not get any sleep or have much to say?"

"Well lupus is tricky," Says my friend Nicky,

"But don't let it fool you. It's always there.
Sometimes it will sneak up on you out of nowhere!

Look at it like this," she said, "It's like a stomach ache, But just because people can't see it doesn't mean the pain is fake.

Or if you fall off your bike with no scratch in sight, does that mean you're not hurt Because you don't have a blood stain on your shirt?"

Does that mean your pain isn't real?
No, because it's not what they see but how you feel ."

Now I see how lupus can be. It's like
falling off my bike without scratching my knee,

Or having a stomach ache that no one can see.
The pain is there. It's just inside of me.

Wow! Now I see that mommy and me
Both have things that people can't see.

So the two of us we will continue to have special times No matter when, where, or what kind!

Whether we're in the house or out in the sun,
Being with mommy is always fun.

No matter how far behind she is in the field trip line
I'll come back and check on her from time to time.
To make sure everything is okay and just fine.

I'll be there even if she's exhausted from a
long day...

Wait don't go !!

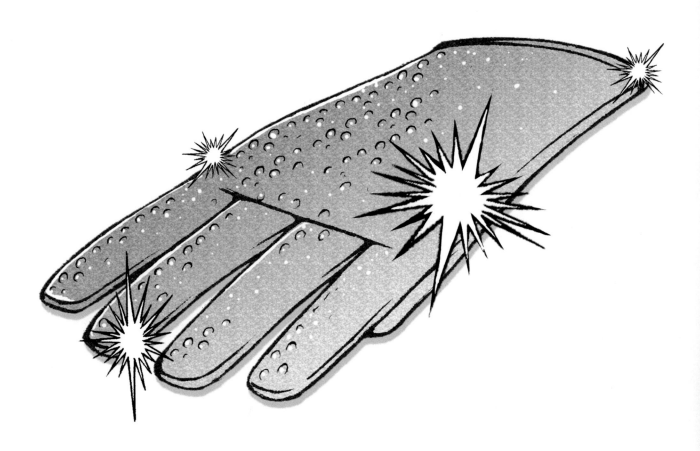

Before I end this story I have one more thing to say:

Me and mommy (daddy) fit together like a hand in a glove,

and Mommy always tells me ...

"The End"

Facts About Lupus

Systemic Lupus Erythematosus (SLE, or lupus) is a chronic autoimmune disease in which a person's immune system mistakenly attacks health tissue.

Lupus can cause life-threatening damage to major organs, such as the kidneys, lungs, heart and central nervous system.

While the disease also affects men and children, 90 % of all those diagnosed are women in their childbearing years.

Women of African-American descent are two-thirds more likely to be diagnosed with lupus.

Also particularly vulnerable women of Hispanic, Asian, and Pacific Islander descent. Lupus is the leading cause of deaths among women with autoimmune diseases.

Lupus cost the nation more than $100 billion a year in direct and indirect medical costs.

The number of Americans affected by lupus is estimated 1,5 million and 16,000 new cases every year.

Although lupus has no cure a person who maintains a healthy lifestyle can go on to live a normal life with lupus.

About the Author

Tammy Anderson had dreams of becoming a grade-school teacher every since she was a child but after her unexpected diagnosis of SLE (Systemic Lupus) that dream seemed almost impossible. At the time of her diagnosis she was only 12 years old, (over 20 years ago) and during the time of her diagnosis there was little to no awareness for Lupus. SLE was new to the medical community, hard to diagnose, and even harder to control. So, with the support from her family and the proper medical attention Tammy persevered met her goal in life, and has now been teaching over 10 years. And because of her passion for teaching she was compelled to write this book and because of her experience with Lupus she was just the right person for the job.

About the Artist

Claude E. Daniel is a great artist that has used his artistic abilities from the early age of five. As a child he grew up in a home with four other siblings. His sisters and brothers would love to play sports, games, and reading any chance that they had but Claude would be happy off to himself sketching whatever came to mind. Always strive to be the best, is a goal he set for himself as a child and has been carried over into his adult life. His work has been displayed at the Tennessee Titans Stadium, various art galleries, Fire Fighters Conventions and in City Hall in Chattanooga TN. "After seeing the passion and love that Tammy had for this project I had no other option except to jump on board and help bring this story to life".

Made in the USA
Coppell, TX
19 November 2019